HAPPY
MARRIAGE lol

A 30-Day He Said/She Said
Devotional for Couples

Jason & Tracy Keech

Happy Pencil Group
St. Francis, Minnesota

Happy Marriage lol
A 30-Day He Said/She Said Devotional For Couples

Copyright © 2018

Editing & Book Description: Kelly Dykstra
Author Photo: Lynn Woolhouse
Cover Art: Tracy Keech

ISBN-13: 978-0-692-05637-0

For Connor and Maddy, our beautiful children.
We love you and we're so proud of you.

ACKNOWLEDGMENTS

HE SAID

Tracy, you are the love of my life. You build me up,
think I'm funny, and tolerate my singing.
You make me better than I am. I love you!

Mom, thank you for giving me a foundation of
faith. I wouldn't be who I am in faith without you.

SHE SAID

Jason, thank you sharing your life with me.
I love you immeasurably! You're my favorite.

Mom & Dad, thank you for showing me what true
love really looks like, and giving me an example
to follow. No one could have done it better.

WE SAID

Eric & Kelly, thank you for all the wisdom,
encouragement, and guidance you have given us.
You are more than our pastors – you're our
best friends. You make us better in every way
because you always point us to Jesus!

JASON & TRACY KEECH

FOREWORD

In January of 2017, a group of us were touring Israel, and one afternoon, we made an unexpected stop in the town of Cana. You may recognize Cana as the place Jesus performed His first miracle. He was a guest at a wedding and saved the day by turning water into wine. Ever since, He has been known for transforming the ordinary into something extraordinary.

Jason and Tracy Keech were with us that day, and the surprise stop was where Jason asked Tracy to marry him all over again. I had the privilege of taking them into a beautiful little chapel and helping them renew their vows during their twentieth year of marriage in the presence of close friends, acquaintances, and other tourists!

Jason and Tracy are two of the wisest, talented, most beautiful souls I've ever known. Jason was the first person I ever baptized at our church. I

3

have watched both of them grow up spiritually and become strong, confident Christ-followers and leaders of others. God has taught them a lot over the years, and they have a phenomenal marriage. Just like Jesus brought the blessing of wine to a wedding, this book will bring the blessing of their wisdom to your relationship.

As you read their words, connect with their stories, and study the Scriptures with them, I believe God will transform your marriage from water into wine. Jesus will take something ordinary and make it extraordinary as you lean in to His wisdom for a beautiful relationship.

May God bless your marriage and grow your love for each other as you let pastors Jason and Tracy share their wisdom with you.

Eric Dykstra
Lead Pastor, The Crossing Church

INTRODUCTION

Here's the deal. We didn't set out to write a book. I know it seems like we did because, well, you're holding it in your hands... but the concepts we wrote about here first began as a class that we taught at our church.

That class was called Happy Marriage 101. However, we soon discovered that when it was hastily written on a dry-erase board, it looks *exactly* like Happy Marriage lol. As in, laugh out loud. Our friend and pastor Kelly will tell you so, because she's the one who saw it first.

Hence, it became lol. And really, that's very fitting if you know us at all. We are definitely more lol than 101. We are just a couple of goofballs who love each other and really like to laugh. In fact, we think that besides Jesus, this is what has held us together as a couple. Being able to laugh with each other keeps the fun in your marriage!

The word "blessed" from Jesus' famous Sermon on the Mount is the word *makarios* in Greek, which means *to be happy or blissful*. This is what we want for you. That you would live *makarios*-ly ever after because your marriage is blessed by God.

What we've written down came from years of trial and error, all kinds of experiences we've shared, and the things we've learned over the 20+ years we've been married. We are still growing and learning and changing, but we're living life happily *TOGETHER*, and that's really what marriage is all about.

So, this book is will be best if you read it *with* your spouse. Do that in whichever way works best for the both of you. Read it aloud together or read it individually, and then talk it about it. We made room for you to write down your thoughts, too. The point is, we'd like you to process what you're learning at the same time so that your bond will be strengthened.

One more thing, we want to encourage each of you to read both the *He Said* and the *She Said* entries each day, as this will help you see things from the other one's perspective.

Have fun!
Jason & Tracy

DAY 1

Matthew 22:37 You must love the LORD your God with all your heart, all your soul, and all your mind.

HE SAID:

Ok, no brainer right? Love God – duh – I can do that. But it's not that easy. Life happens, kids show up, bills come in, stress from work and relationships creep in, and suddenly you find that a day, week, or a month have gone by, and you haven't prayed, or read your Bible, or gone to church. You start to notice that the things of God are sliding to the back burner of your life.

If you really want to get the "loving your wife" thing done right, you have to start with the "loving God with all you have and do" thing. Begin to love Him with a no-holds-barred, give-it-all kind of love first.

This is why we wanted to do a devotional –

because of the word *devotion*. What is your life devoted to? That's easy to answer – just think about which things you spend most of your time and energy pursuing. I think for most of us, it might be work and putting food on the table. Worst-case scenario, you have an addiction issue, so drugs, alcohol, porn, or some other unhealthy thing rules your life right now.

I want you to be honest with yourself in this moment. Is God getting the best of your love, or is it something else? If you give Him your best first, it always seems like everything else falls into place. I really want to love my wife well; I want that relationship to be amazing. But it has to start with God first always.

Write down some ways you need to put God first in your life right now, and then ask Him to help you make Him a priority. He can do a lot to help you, if you are willing.

SHE SAID:

Jason is very important to me. I don't think there are adequate words to convey how much I love him and how much he means to me. I rely on him for so much. He comforts me when I'm feeling down. He loves me even though he knows all my flaws. And he can really make me laugh. He's funny. Like, super funny. Like Jim Carrey funny, but wayyyyy more handsome.

We kind of have a running joke about how many times people have told me, "You must laugh all the time!" This is exceptionally hilarious when he tells a total eye-roll of a joke, and we will both sarcastically say, "You must laugh allllll the time." Really, I just adore this man and all our inside jokes and the time we get to spend together. He's my tall drink of water! I'm grateful I get to do life with him.

But Jason can't be my Savior or my God. I love him more than every other person on this planet, but I don't love him more than I love Jesus. If I did, everything in my life would be out of whack. If I put Jason up on a pedestal, he will eventually let me down because he can't be perfect.

Let this verse remind you who should be first place in your life. Love God with all your heart, soul, and mind, and everything else will fall into place. What does this look like? Worship God, serve Him, and spend time in His Word. Talk to Him in prayer.

Your relationship with God is the most important relationship you could ever have! Today, commit to loving Him first.

DAY 2

Mark 10:7-9 This explains why a man leaves his father and mother and is joined to his wife, and the two are united into one. Since they are no longer two but one, let no one split apart what God has joined together.

HE SAID:

Ok, here is the deal, I was raised as a total Mama's boy. I was my mom's only boy, and I got away with stuff my sisters didn't. I was treated way different. I honestly don't think I ever cleaned my room growing up – my mom would do it for me. When I moved out, my mom still did all my laundry for a couple years. To be honest, that's a little embarrassing, but it was just the way it was.

When I was first married, it was not uncommon for me to have discussions with my mom about my relationship with my wife. That's all fine and good, but sometimes it turned into a complaint session.

13

As you can probably guess, this didn't work in my favor when it came to my marriage. According to this verse, men, we leave mom and dad and become one. So what I was doing was willingly bringing my mom into my marriage. Ummm, that's not good.

When you say, "I do," you are saying the most important person in your world is now your spouse. As soon as I figured this out, I no longer went to my mom to be my sounding board. When I decided not to vent to anyone about my relationship and just figure it out with my wife face-to-face, we got so much closer! I can't say this enough, you have both become one. There is no more "just me", there is only "my wife and me". If you can start to think this way, you will start to become so much closer. What relationship do you need to reduce in order to elevate your marriage to a place above any other relationship on earth? Write it down and ask Christ to remind you to put your wife first!

SHE SAID:

Jason and I were pretty young when we got married. He was 22, and I was 21. This means we still had some growing up to do individually. We also had some growing to do together. This can be tough when you've been used to relying on your parents for most things. But when you get together, you are choosing to walk away from the past and start a new life together. When we got married, the most important person in my life was no longer mom or dad - it was Jason. We leave the past behind, and step into the future together.

It makes me think of this quote from *Lion King*:

Pumbaa: *It's like my buddy Timon always says, "You got to put your behind in your past."*
Timon: *No, no, no. Amateur. Sit down before you hurt yourself. It's, "You got to put your past behind you."*

Is there something or someone from your past that's causing a split in your relationship? Maybe it isn't even something from the past. Kids and friendships and work and to-do lists are always fighting for our attention, too.

This verse tells us not to let anyone separate us. Separation can be a sneak attack. Jason and I have noticed that when we get home at the end of a long day, we each tend to grab our phones as we veg out on the couch, paying attention to Candy Crush or Instagram instead of each other.

Today, see if you can figure out what it is that keeps you from being the couple that God joined together, and make a plan to be one again.

HE THOUGHT:

_____
_____
_____
_____
_____
_____
_____
_____
_____
_____
_____
_____
_____
_____

SHE THOUGHT:

_____
_____
_____
_____
_____
_____
_____
_____
_____
_____
_____
_____
_____
_____

DAY 3

*Amos 3:3 Can two people walk together
without agreeing on the direction?*

HE SAID:

Have you ever participated in one of those three-legged races? Those are really hard. Basically you tie one of your legs to a partner's leg and try to beat everyone else to the finish line. Mostly it's difficult because you and the person you are sharing a leg with haven't had time to practice. At least you both know the way you need to go.

Marriage is like this. Basically at the beginning, you both are agreeing to come together and do life together as "one". This is hard because you've spent your whole life so far doing life for just one person – yourself. Then suddenly you are sharing your life with someone else. You "tie the knot" and start hopping toward the finish line.

The greatest difficulty often times isn't the actual moving, it's figuring out which way we should go. You see in marriage, unlike a three-legged race, you can't always see the finish line. If you both aren't sure where the finish line is, you can spend a lot of time spinning in circles and going nowhere. This gets exhausting and can end in frustration and conflict.

If you want to see your relationship move in a positive direction, you have to have a finish line or at least a direction to move in. Talk about where you are going together. How do you want your career to go, where do you want to live, and how do you want to raise your kids? When you start to have conversations and agree about the way you want to go, you will see your marriage succeed because you have agreed on the direction!

SHE SAID:

Did you read the verse? Ok, good. Now picture a man who is 6'6" and a woman who is 5'4" trying to walk in sync together. This is us – Jason and me. I take at least two steps for every one of his long-legged strides! It's hard enough for me to keep up with him on a normal day, much less when we're in a hurry. You can lol now – it's ok.

Now let's picture something even more ridiculous. Actually, it would be impossible. If we both wanted to walk to church, but he started going west and I only walked east, we would never arrive together. (To be honest, I don't know if either one of us would arrive because I'm kind of directionally-challenged.)

The point is: You can't walk in opposite directions and expect to end up at the same destination!

It is the same with the direction of your lives. If you want to want to arrive at the same destination — paying off your debt, buying a home, saving for vacation, raising successful kids — you've got to be on the same page. This takes something called compromise. I know that's not a fun word for everyone, but if that's what it takes to get to the dream together, it's so worth it!

Today, think about how you can compromise to make sure you're walking in the same direction.

HE THOUGHT:

_____

_____

_____

_____

_____

_____

_____

_____

_____

_____

_____

_____

SHE THOUGHT:

_____

_____

_____

_____

_____

_____

_____

_____

_____

_____

_____

_____

DAY 4

Ephesians 5:21-25 And further, submit to one another out of reverence for Christ. For wives, this means submit to your husbands as to the Lord. For a husband is the head of his wife as Christ is the head of the church. He is the Savior of his body, the church. As the church submits to Christ, so you wives should submit to your husbands in everything. For husbands, this means love your wives, just as Christ loved the church. He gave up his life for her...

HE SAID:

Ok, I just need to say that as a man, the word submit really has a negative connotation for me. When I think about it, I think of when I was a kid and I used to watch wrestling with my dad. (You know where I'm going if you grew up in the 80's.) There was always a hold that was impossible for the wrestler to escape. Maybe it was the claw, or a chokehold, or the scissor leg lock. You know that the moment those holds were applied, it was only a matter of time before the opponent would tap out, or "submit."

For men in particular we think, "If I submit, it means I lose." Most men don't like to lose – we want to dominate in all that we do. I mean, I hate it if someone passes me while I'm driving on a two-lane road. It feels like I am losing the race. That other guy just beat me somehow – that's not a good feeling. So when some people read this verse and see the word "submit", their stomach turns a little. We have associated it with losing, and it has become a negative thing rather than a good thing.

So, I just want remind you of a couple things: First, your wife is not your opponent. You are not in a contest to be the best human or the best partner. When you got together, you became a team. You aren't out to beat the other – you are together. When one of you is doing well, you both are. Get out of the competition mindset.

Second, submission is a good thing. It means I want what you want. I am happy when you are happy. I don't have to always do things my way. I am a very stubborn person who really likes to set the tone and do things my way. But here is the thing: I can be wrong. Sometimes there can be a better way to do things. I want to challenge you with this. What if you started to take time to consider that maybe the way your wife does things is better than the way you want to do them? What if you took time to at least consider her opinion and listen to what she wants? I say this a lot, and I know you have probably heard it, too: happy wife, happy life. It is so true. When I submit to my wife and go out of my way to not be stubborn and be more considerate, she is happier, and so am I. Be willing to give up your way. Write down one way you need to submit today.

SHE SAID:

Wait wait wait. Hold up a minute. Submi....say whaaaat? Yikes. That word really freaks people out for some reason. Maybe it's because you think that submitting to someone else (especially wives to your husbands) is some kind of archaic concept reserved for, well, old-fashioned types. Surely nobody in this century would ever think this was a good idea.

BUT! Read that first part again. Submit to *one another*. Ok, now we're talking. In my opinion, this is THE verse that changed our marriage. Life

25

before this verse was a constant battle to get my own way. We used to argue about everything - whose turn it was to do the dishes or change the diaper or scrub the toilet. Then we began to not just *read about*, but also *actually apply* the "submit to one another" principle. It was revolutionary.

Is it his turn to do the dishes? Maybe. But if I just do them, they'll be done, and we can enjoy our evening. That's waayyyyy better than arguing about it for 15 minutes, then stewing about it for the next two hours.

As I began to submit to Jason's will and him to mine, the arguments ceased. (Not completely. I mean, gosh, we aren't perfect.) The secret is, we were both on board with this plan. He stepped up, and so did I, and we are happier now. Stress and strife disappear when you humble yourselves and submit to each other. Try it, you'll see.

HE THOUGHT:

_____

_____

_____

_____

_____

_____

_____

_____

_____

_____

_____

_____

_____

SHE THOUGHT:

_____

_____

_____

_____

_____

_____

_____

_____

_____

_____

_____

_____

_____

DAY 5

John 15:12 This is my commandment:
Love each other in the same way I have loved you.

HE SAID:

I want you to think of the most messed-up person you ever met. And when I say messed-up, I mean *messed-up*. Maybe they were mean to you. Maybe they used to beat you up everyday. I don't know who your person is, but picture them in your mind. Can you see them? Now in your mind (not in person, that would be weird...) walk up to them and give them the biggest hug you can muster. Look them in the eye and tell them you love them.

I know that is probably the weirdest thing you have ever done, but this is how Christ loves you. He sees your dysfunction and how messed up you are, and He just loves you. It doesn't even matter that you have flaws. That's awesome! I love that about Him. He commands us to do the same, and that is

29

the scary part.

We are called to love like He loves. He is so perfect. He never made a mistake, and yet He loves us. I don't know how your marriage is going. Maybe it's a red-hot mess, and you got this book hoping something would help because you feel like you are just done. But I know this: without love, no marriage can succeed.

Maybe today is the day you sit down and look your spouse in the eye, and say, "I love you." Don't ask for anything in return or worry about the past or all the things they have messed up or said to hurt you. Just choose to love them. *Choose it.* It probably won't fix all your problems, but it is a really good place to start. The Gospel – the Good News of Christ – always starts with love. "For God so loved the world..." Start there, and you just might start to see some progress in your marriage.

SHE SAID:

I loved Show and Tell day in elementary school. Show and Tell was awesome because it meant you didn't just get to talk about that amazing trip to the ocean you took over summer vacation, you got to show your peers proof of your trip by way of your killer new seashell collection.

If we are to love each other in the same way Jesus loves us, we must ask ourselves, "Well, how does He love us?" It's a fair question. We can find the answer all over Scripture, but I think Romans 5:8 says it all: *But God <u>demonstrates</u> his own love for us in this: While we were still sinners, Christ died for us.*

God didn't allow His love to be theoretical; He gave it an action step. He didn't just tell you He loved you, He demonstrated it. God looked at you as you were trapped in your state of doing the wrong thing, and He exhibited the greatest act of love of all time to set you free. He actually *proved* His love by dying for you.

God's Word *tells* us of His love, and He *showed* us at the cross.

I can tell Jason over and over again how much I love him. I could repeat myself endlessly, and that would be nice I guess, but over time, it would just go in one ear and out the other. But if I put action behind it? That would be powerful. What if I demonstrated my love in a tangible way that meant something more than my words could convey? Maybe I will cook his favorite meal for dinner tonight or surprise him in some completely unexpected way, like willingly taking him to Cabela's to buy more fishing gear that he doesn't need. I'm sure you can think of lots of ways to show your husband you love him... *if you know what I mean.*

This is, I believe, what it means to love each other in the same way God loved us – to show and tell. How can you do that today?

HE THOUGHT:

_____

_____

_____

_____

_____

_____

_____

_____

_____

_____

_____

_____

_____

SHE THOUGHT:

_____

_____

_____

_____

_____

_____

_____

_____

_____

_____

_____

_____

_____

DAY 6

Ecclesiastes 4:9 Two people are better off than one, for they can help each other succeed.

HE SAID:

Ok, so I like to do things on my own sometimes. I am a typical guy. Pull yourself up by your bootstraps and self-made and all that jazz. But here is what I have learned over the years: no one can really succeed on their own. The fact is God made man, then looked at him and said that it was not good for him to be alone. Honestly, marriage is a ton of work. You have to put in a lot of hours and invest in your relationship to make it work. But being alone is so much harder. If you catch yourself wishing you were single or getting tired of the work it takes to succeed in your relationship, remember your motivation for getting together in the first place.

Being alone sucks. I love being able to have someone with whom I can celebrate all the accomplishments in life. In fact, my wife sometimes thinks it's funny when I celebrate silly stuff like fixing the lawnmower or installing a new floor. But I love that I have someone to celebrate with!

One of my favorite things is having my wife to do life with me. I love talking about all the stuff only she and I can talk about. We have developed and worked out a trust over the last two decades. It's awesome! Men, you were not meant to do it alone. Always be grateful you have a partner to do life with. When I'm not parenting well, she picks up the slack. When I feel down about one of my sermons, she encourages me to keep swinging for the fences.

You will succeed so much more in life when you embrace the helper that God has placed in your corner. He brought her into your life because he knew you would succeed together. How can you be more open to her help in your life? Write it down.

SHE SAID:

"How did you two meet?"

It's a fun question to ask people when you're just getting to know them. Jason and I met in his driveway through mutual friends. His, who was on leave from the Air Force, and mine, who was interested in aforementioned friend. The story is that Jason saw me get out of the car and immediately went inside and changed his shirt to impress me. Awwwww!

But this isn't where our story began. Our "once upon a time" was written by God and not by chance. He decided to bring the two of us together in that moment, and He had a purpose for doing so, even if we didn't discover it until many years later.

I believe there's something good that God designed for the both of you to accomplish in unison, side-by-side and hand-in-hand. For what reason did God make sure you two met and fell in love? What is your purpose? Pray and ask God why He thought you'd be better together, then help each other succeed!

HE THOUGHT:

_____

_____

_____

_____

_____

_____

_____

_____

_____

_____

_____

_____

SHE THOUGHT:

_____

_____

_____

_____

_____

_____

_____

_____

_____

_____

_____

_____

_____

DAY 7

1 Peter 5:8 Stay alert! Watch out for your great enemy, the devil. He prowls around like a roaring lion, looking for someone to devour.

HE SAID:

The Usual Suspects is a great movie. I don't know if you have seen it, but one of my favorite quotes from the movie is, "The greatest trick the devil ever pulled was convincing the world he didn't exist."

I really think this is so true. So many people don't want to believe that there is an entity whose sole purpose is to make your life hell. In fact, I have even heard people say things like, "God must hate me." Man, that is so crazy! It makes me so sad that people would view God that way.

So first off, let me say that God unequivocally loves you – I have no doubt in my mind. If you do, think

39

of this: He sent His one and only Son on a rescue mission for you, because of His love. Second, I think it is scary as heck that people don't realize we have an enemy. There is an enemy of your soul – whether you believe in Christ or not – who just wants you to be wrecked. He wants to destroy everything good in your life, including every relationship.

I grew up watching *G.I. Joe*. (What can I say? I'm an 80's kid.) On the show, they always said, "Now you know, and knowing is half the battle." See, you can't fight an enemy if you don't even know you are at war.

Remember the movie *The Matrix*? Everyone was going about their normal lives, but the truth is they were all held captive by an enemy and didn't even know it. Once they realized it, they began to fight. They refused to let the enemy steal what doesn't belong to him.

You have an enemy. He wants to steal your joy, your peace, and every relationship you have, even your relationship with God. Refuse to let this happen! Realize that sometimes the fight you are in with your wife, isn't really with your wife! When you recognize that, you'll start to win. You'll start to have joy and peace again, and you'll start to experience true love. What are some ways in which the enemy tries to devour you? Write them down, and pray that God will help you win these battles!

SHE SAID:

Imagine you're in the jungle being stalked by a lion. What would you do? I know I would keep tabs on that lion and make sure I didn't go into his territory, for one thing. I would stay far away from any traps he set that would make me his next victim. I most definitely wouldn't tease that lion or pull his tail or get within his reach.

Here's the thing: you *are* being hunted. The devil wants to devour you and everything you care about. As the great theologian Axl Rose says, "You're in the jungle, baby!" Eek! Now what?

Read the verse again. God tells us to stay alert. The dictionary definition tells us that to be alert means we are "quick to notice any unusual and potentially dangerous or difficult circumstances; to remain vigilant." So keep your eyes peeled and look for areas in your marriage where the devil is always trying to attack. Maybe it's with your intimacy or your finances or some kind of unexpected anger or resentment rising up.

Once we can see the attack, then what do we do? I love God's Word because it doesn't just give us warning signals like this one; it also provides solutions. And the Bible says to resist the devil and he will flee from you (James 4:7). Resist the devil wherever he is trying to attack.

He attacks intimacy through porn and other sexual sin. Resist that! Run away! He attacks our finances when we don't choose to put God first. But once we choose to place our finances in God's hands, guess what? The devil can't have a foothold in that area anymore. Are you harboring an unresolved resentment? The devil is winning in that area because he uses it to cause division. You can fight back through forgiveness.

Be alert today and resist that lion. Don't let him devour you or your marriage. Take some time to identify the ways in which your marriage is being attacked, then pray against it together.

HE THOUGHT:

_____
_____
_____
_____
_____
_____
_____
_____
_____
_____
_____
_____
_____
_____

SHE THOUGHT:

_____
_____
_____
_____
_____
_____
_____
_____
_____
_____
_____
_____
_____
_____

DAY 8

1 John 4:19 We love each other
because he loved us first.

HE SAID:

I love this verse because it really takes the pressure off of me. Ever wonder where love comes from? It literally comes from Christ! We don't have to fake it 'til we make it; Christ gives us His love, and we give it to others as a gift. It is the original gift that keeps on giving.

Most of the men I know are not real naturals at love. I mean think about it – we just aren't wired that way. We are rough-around-the-edges, tough, leathery, and not really all that good at expressing our emotions. And you know what? That can be good. I mean, think about it: if you were an emotional wreck every time you had to do something, your wife would roll her eyes at you all the time.

45

One of our daughter Maddy's favorite things to do is to watch my eyes when I watch a sad part of a movie. She is checking to see if I am going to cry. She loves to see her dad express emotion in some way. One of the things that can be hard for me, and men in general, is showing their emotions, especially sadness and love.

Here is the good news: because He loves us first, we can love. You don't have to try and make it up. When I remember that Christ loves me *all the muches* (as Connor would say when he was little), I can love. It just flows out of me when I accept His love. When I think of the only perfect One ever and His love for me, it helps me to be more loving.

I want to help you *think* differently today. When we *think* Christ loves us, it changes us. Your belief determines your outcomes. If I believe a road is closed, I don't drive that way. If I believe that Christ loves me, I don't live in wonder and fear and guilt, I live in love. Therefore, I am able to love people better, including my wife.

I want you to take a second and pray for God to reveal His love for you. I want you to believe and feel it, and then live knowing you are loved so that you can love.

SHE SAID:

I used to think I wasn't worthy of God's love. I did so many stupid things growing up that I believed He could not possibly overlook them all. I was a typical party girl, and I made some really bad decisions, many of which were the direct result of not knowing my own worth.

Do you know yours?

Do you know that if you've given Jesus the leadership of your life, you are now His child? (Romans 8:15)

Do you know He has made you brand new? (2 Corinthians 5:17)

Do you know God lives in you? (1 John 4:4)

Do you know you are righteous?
(2 Corinthians 5:21)

Do you know you are forgiven? (Ephesians 1:7)

Do you know GOD LOVES YOU? (John 3:16)

Our love for each other begins with the compassionate, awe-inspiring, unfailing love of

47

God. We can only truly love another person the way God loves them when we have received His love for ourselves.

Love wasn't just a great theoretical idea God thought up one day. No! God *IS* love (1 John 4:8). If you don't have God, you don't have love. You might have a worldly version of love, but you are missing out on something spectacular.

I think this is why when Jason and I finally surrendered to Him, our marriage was completely turned around. It all begins and ends with Jesus. It's all about Him. If you want more love in your marriage, start with the Savior.

Today, write down a prayer to thank God for His unfathomable love.

HE THOUGHT:

_____
_____
_____
_____
_____
_____
_____
_____
_____
_____
_____
_____
_____

SHE THOUGHT:

_____
_____
_____
_____
_____
_____
_____
_____
_____
_____
_____
_____
_____

DAY 9

Colossians 3:14 Above all, clothe yourselves with love, which binds us all together in perfect harmony.

HE SAID:

Have you noticed that there seems to be a massive shortage of love in the world? I honestly think most people seem to clothe themselves in complaining and negativity rather than love and positivity. We say this all the time, "You can't have a positive life with a negative mind." You also can't have a loving relationship if you aren't showing the love.

One of my favorite things is getting new clothes. I don't get them very often, and, when I do, I tend to wear them a lot. I'll wear new shoes all over the house because I love them. Plus, they haven't been outside yet, so they aren't messing anything up. I will wear new shirts or pants every week when I first get them.

51

We are to be this way with love. Wear it all the time, everywhere we go, showing the love, just like our new clothes.

Think of how great your relationship would be – how close you would be – if you were always showing the love to your wife. Don't be one of those guys who says to himself, "She knows I love her." No, say it and spray it! Wear your love for her. This doesn't mean you have to be super sappy or mushy; just intentionally choose to go a little bit out of your way every day to make sure that she knows you love her.

When you do that, you become so close. Stupid arguments become less frequent, and there's more peace in your house. I want to challenge you right now to find ways to show more love. You might be really good at it – great! Do it more. This is the one thing that will bind you together and bring harmony into your marriage.

Honestly, this is why my wife and I get along so well and have been married for over twenty years. We never doubt our love for one another. I want you to write down some ways that you can wear or show your love more and more to your wife.

SHE SAID:

I love lots of different types of music. You will find everything from Etta James to Metallica to Coldplay to Adele in my collection. But the music I love most of all contains harmony. Harmony is when all the voices are singing different notes, but they complement each other perfectly. Bands like the Eagles and Mumford & Sons do this so well. I'm a total sucker for good harmonies!

This verse talks about how we can achieve perfect harmony in a non-musical way. It tells us that love is the secret ingredient. It is what binds us. Love is the glue that holds our marriages together. And we should clothe ourselves in it. Other translations of the Bible say to put on love and wear it around. When we do this, we perfectly complement each other. That's beautiful!

I was trying to think of something I wear every single day so I could compare it to love. Something like, "You wear underwear every day, so wear love like you wear underwear! Never leave home without it." But that was kind of dumb. Then it dawned on me. Something (besides underwear) that I wear every day without fail is my wedding ring. In fact, I never take it off. When I look at it there on my finger, it reminds me that there was a day I promised to love and to cherish, for better for worse, for richer for poorer, in sickness and in health. And just like I never stop wearing the symbol of that covenant, may I never cease to wear the love that binds us together.

Do you feel like you're out of tune with your spouse? Maybe it's because you forgot to put on love today. It's not too late to put it on in order to live in harmony! Today, make a conscious decision to shake off the stuff that doesn't matter and clothe yourself with love.

HE THOUGHT:

_____
_____
_____
_____
_____
_____
_____
_____
_____
_____
_____
_____
_____

SHE THOUGHT:

_____
_____
_____
_____
_____
_____
_____
_____
_____
_____
_____
_____
_____
_____

DAY 10

*Ephesians 4:2-3 Always be humble and gentle.
Be patient with each other, making allowance
for each other's faults because of your love.
Make every effort to keep yourselves united in
the Spirit, binding yourselves together with peace.*

HE SAID:

I feel like talking like William Shatner right now. *Peace – the final frontier...* Sometimes peace can be a foreign concept, am I right? I mean think of the world we live in. It's loud, full of war, full of strife, full of constant interruptions. At work it's stressful, at home the kids are loud. And yet, we are to be bound together by peace.

Easy peasy, right? I think the key thing in this verse is to stay united in the Spirit. This means you need to have the Spirit of God holding your relationship together. I feel like Clark Griswold when I try and keep the peace on my own in my house (you know, from *Christmas Vacation*). Clark tries to create the perfect Christmas experience, and he fails miserably. It turns into the worst-case scenario. That's what happens when we try to achieve peace in our relationships by our own strength.

We need God to give us His peace. This is what Christ gives us – His peace! For my wife and I it looks like this: we pray together. When was the last time you prayed for or with your wife? Pray that she would feel better, or even just before you eat dinner. When we don't pray together, it's hard for peace to rule in our heart, because we are not connecting with the Spirit.

Worship together. When was the last time you both worshiped Jesus together? Honestly, I think our marriage is as good as it is because we go to church every week and have for the last fourteen plus years. You might be thinking, "Well you have to, you're the pastor." I wasn't always a pastor! Still, I led my family and made sure that we were in the House of God every week. When you make worship a priority, He begins to bind you together in peace!

I have so much more I could write, I could fill a book on this topic alone. I want to you to write a commitment to God to worship weekly, to lead your wife, and see your marriage thrive. I believe this is how you will see peace in your relationship.

SHE SAID:

It takes me one cup of coffee, some quiet time, and about an hour to feel awake in the morning. It takes about all of five minutes before Jason starts belting out whatever rock ballad is stuck in his brain.

And me? Well, I'm not perfect. I have been known to become easily irritated over the smallest of annoyances. I can also be demanding at times, especially when I'm ordering him to laugh at my really corny jokes.

These are the moments in marriage that tend to try our patience. I'm not saying his air-guitar-playing inner rock star is one of his faults, but how I respond to one of his concerts is very telling as to whether or not I'm practicing patience and making allowance for him to just be, well, HIM.

I love this verse! It gives us step-by-step directions for getting along with each other. Be humble – you're not perfect. Be gentle – he's not trying to be annoying. Be patient and make allowances for each other. Why? Because you love each other! Stay united – you're on the same team. Your unity binds you together and creates a peaceful atmosphere. (Yes, even if he's still singing at the top of his lungs.)

Sometimes all I need to do is pour another cup of coffee, smile, and thank God that he's mine and I'm his. How can you make allowance for your partner's faults today?

HE THOUGHT:

_____

_____

_____

_____

_____

_____

_____

_____

_____

_____

_____

_____

_____

SHE THOUGHT:

_____

_____

_____

_____

_____

_____

_____

_____

_____

_____

_____

_____

_____

DAY 11

James 1:19 You must all be quick to listen, slow to speak, and slow to get angry.

HE SAID:

I'm not going to lie – I am not a really big fan of this verse. That's mainly because I can get angry pretty quickly, and talking is way easier than listening. I think most men struggle to be good listeners because it takes a lot of time and energy. We just want to jump to the solution to the problem so we don't have to mess with it anymore. We want to check the issue off our mental "to-do" list so we can feel some peace. This is where we miss the boat. Most women need to talk about the problem and express all of their feelings so they can feel like they have it off their own mental "to-do" list. Therein lies conflict, a lot of conflict. I have known that my wife likes to talk about her problems without me just offering a solution for many years now. But I *still* consistently stop

63

listening and jump straight to offering a solution, much to her chagrin.

Men, you need to shut up. Just shut your yapper and listen. Be slow to speak, and don't get frustrated because you can see a simple solution that she isn't ready to accept. 90% of the time, it is not about a solution. I'm serious! When your wife is frustrated and wants to talk to you, the best thing you can do is listen. And I mean actually listen. Shut the TV off, stash the cell phone somewhere, get the glazed look out of your eyes, and listen.

You can do it, but it is going to take practice. You have to fight the urge to give your opinion. Here is my suggestion for you today. After you have listened, don't even offer a solution, just offer to pray for her. Hold hands with her or just hug her close and ask Christ to be her comfort. Ask Him to be the solution to the problem. Wow, how much better would your relationship be if you just did that? Ask God right now to help make you a better listener, and write that prayer down today.

SHE SAID:

This verse is like Conflict Resolution 101 with Jesus, and I cannot possibly do these three things on a consistent basis without His help. My guess is that you and I are similar in this regard. So let's use an imaginary scenario to make practical examples we all can learn from. Here's the situation: someone forgot to change the laundry load, and now all the clothes smell musty.

Quick to listen. Communication is not just talking; it is also receiving the information that is being conveyed. So many times, I rush to be understood and I don't pause to understand. Today I will choose to close my mouth and open my ears to actually hear what is being communicated to me. If all I do is loudly express my annoyance at having to restart the laundry load, I won't hear him say he thought I had already changed it. So then I won't have the opportunity to be gracious about a normal misunderstanding.

Slow to speak. This kind of goes along with the first one, but I want to give it just a twist. When I'm slow to speak, it means I will choose my words carefully and not just blurt out the first thing that pops into my head. And that's a good thing, because (I'm gonna be really real here) sometimes the first thing that pops into my head isn't very nice. When I'm slow to speak, it means I remember that my words carry weight, and once they pop out of my mouth, they aren't easily forgotten. Besides,

I'm better than that kind of behavior. And you are, too! (Side note: repenting of the not-nice thoughts is also a good idea.)

Slow to get angry. I believe this is what happens when we practice numbers one and two well. Good communication is the key to remaining calm in stressful or annoying situations.

And just one more thing…

When I think about some of the fights we've had in the past, I can't even remember what got me so heated in the first place. Moral of the story: musty clothes aren't worth the trouble. There. Now you've had conflict resolution training from Jesus. Go put it into practice!

HE THOUGHT:

_____
_____
_____
_____
_____
_____
_____
_____
_____
_____
_____
_____
_____
_____

SHE THOUGHT:

_____
_____
_____
_____
_____
_____
_____
_____
_____
_____
_____
_____
_____
_____

HAPPY MARRIAGE lol

DAY 12

*Psalm 143:8 Let me hear of your unfailing love
each morning, for I am trusting you.
Show me where to walk, for I give myself to you.*

HE SAID:

This is such a great verse. I think it speaks to our human need to know that we are loved. This is a prayer really – asking God to reassure you and to reaffirm His love. But so much more than that, it is a commitment to God. "I give myself to you." Marriage reflects this aspect of a relationship with God. In marriage, you are giving yourself to someone else. You are saying, "I trust you." This is no small thing. It is SO hard for people to do this, to give themselves away.

It means giving up control. It means having faith in someone else. It is really easy for me to trust myself because I already know my strengths and I know all the ways I will let myself down. When I trust someone else, the letdowns are usually a surprise, so over time I develop defense mechanisms to keep myself from being let down.

I have two questions for you today. First, if you have never given yourself to God, you can do that today. He wants to show you the way through life and be there with you always, but you have to choose Him.

Have you given your life to Christ? You can pray this simple prayer: "Christ, thank You for dying for me, I want You to lead me and forgive my past. I give myself to You." If you prayed that, congratulations! I believe that is the best prayer you can pray. Ask Him each day to affirm His unfailing love in your life.

My second question is: have you given yourself fully to your wife? Have you trusted her? Commit to her and your relationship. Give yourself fully to her; don't hold anything back. If you do these two things, I really believe your marriage is going to be something so amazing.

If you did that today, write it down. Write down the date so you can look back and remind yourself that you have committed yourself to God and to your wife. That is a big deal! I'm proud of you.

SHE SAID:

We live in Minnesota, where the winters can be brutally cold. It is not uncommon for everything to freeze, and because I'm writing this in January, I am painfully aware of how arctic it can be in this state that I will never ever want to leave. (Sorry Jason, you'll have to pray God changes my heart in order to get me to move somewhere that's consistently over 100 degrees every day in the summer. That's just too hot!)

One thing Jason always makes sure to do is throw ice melt down on the steps and sidewalk in the winter. But even ice melt doesn't always help in -23 degree wind chill. (I'm not even making that up. That was the wind chill today. Brrrr!)

Since we commute to work together, we leave the house at the same time in the morning. I've noticed He always goes out the door first, and then he turns around to stand guard and keep me steady so I don't fall down and break something. It's really sweet. As he leads the way to the car, he points out potentially dangerous hazards all along the way. He shows me where to walk, and I trust him to keep me safe.

This is what God does for us – He guides our steps

to keep us safe. This verse reminds me to look to God each morning for a confirmation of His unfailing love, and to trust Him with the steps He wants me to take. But I can't know what they are unless I listen to His voice – just like I listen to Jason as he warns me to be careful for the slippery spots.

Today, ask God to remind you of His love for you, then write a prayer of trust and ask God to guide your steps today.

HE THOUGHT:

_____
_____
_____
_____
_____
_____
_____
_____
_____
_____
_____
_____
_____

SHE THOUGHT:

_____
_____
_____
_____
_____
_____
_____
_____
_____
_____
_____
_____
_____

JASON & TRACY KEECH

DAY 13

Ecclesiastes 9:9 Live happily with the woman you love through all the meaningless days of life that God has given you under the sun. The wife God gives you is your reward for all your earthly toil.

HE SAID:

When I first got married – mind you this was before I really followed Jesus (B.C. Before Christ) – I used to call my wife stuff like "my old lady", or "the ball and chain". Wow, I really missed what a blessing she was from the Lord. For real! This verse, and Scripture in general, says that she is a reward and a blessing from God. I used to have a mindset that she slowed me down or wasn't beneficial to me. At least, that's the way my words portrayed her.

I had to change the way I spoke about her when I came to Christ and I realized what a gift she is. I hope today you realize what a gift your wife is. You are not the man you are without the gift God has

75

blessed you with. She is your reward, not your 401k or your Christmas bonus. What if today you started to speak only of your wife as a blessing and a reward?

If you choose to view her as a positive in your life, your relationship is going to be so much better! When I started to speak positively about Tracy, calling her my beautiful wife and not complaining to anyone about her ever, my relationship got so much better. In fact, I would say it got hotter... *if you know what I mean.* If you want to have a great relationship, you have to think about it positively and speak about it positively. She is your reward and your blessing, talk about her as such and treat her that way, and you will be so much happier!

And remember, since this verse says our days are meaningless and our reward is our wife, maybe we should be making her the priority, and not our careers or other things that don't mean as much.

SHE SAID:

I've had some amazing examples of marriage to look up to throughout my life. My dad passed away in 2006, just a few days after he and my mom celebrated their 36th wedding anniversary. In all my years growing up, I honestly can't think of one time I ever saw them argue. Seriously. Not even one. And they spent a lot of time together. Not necessarily going on dates all the time, but just being in the same room together – him watching the Minnesota Twins or Vikings and her reading a book. They loved each other so unconditionally, it is crazy!

Another marriage example I had to look up to was my Papa Bud and Grandma Ruth. They were married for 67 years. One time Jason and I were at their house visiting, and they told us about their morning ritual. Every day they would play three games of cribbage, and then they'd write the name of whoever won the best two out of three games on the calendar in the kitchen. I love the fact that they were still enjoying each other's company during their great-grandparent years.

The reason I think both of these marriages were successful is because they took time to live *happily* together. They enjoyed being around each other. They found things they loved to do together, and they took the time to connect. Listen, your days on earth might feel meaningless and full of toil, but you also have the reward of someone to share your life with. So, be happy in it!

Growing up with these examples taught me so much about how to love my husband. And I just have to say, your kids are learning how to love their future spouse by watching you, just like I learned by watching my parents. Will your kids have great marriages because of the way they saw you treat and love your husband or wife? I hope mine do.

Think of some things you love to do together, and set the time aside to do them. Those are the things that matter most!

Now think of some ways you can leave a legacy of love for future generations to follow, and write them down.

HE THOUGHT:

_____
_____
_____
_____
_____
_____
_____
_____
_____
_____
_____
_____
_____

SHE THOUGHT:

_____
_____
_____
_____
_____
_____
_____
_____
_____
_____
_____
_____
_____
_____

DAY 14

*1 Corinthians 13:4-5 Love is patient and kind.
Love is not jealous or boastful or proud or rude.
It does not demand its own way. It is not irritable,
and it keeps no record of being wronged.*

HE SAID:

Ok, so this is a tough one for me. Patience is a virtue, and it seems like it's in short supply. Often times we use up all our patience on everyone else in our lives and when we get home to our wife and family, our patience tank is on empty, and kindness is running low. So how do we keep it full? How do we not get irritated? How do we resist using this verse as ammunition in an argument if she mentions that you always leave the seat up or your socks on the floor? "Um, dear, remember love keeps no records of wrong..."

Scripture says God is love. So for me, if I am running out of love and patience and kindness, it

81

might mean I haven't been going to the source much. Have you ever run out of gas? I mean, that is a bad feeling, right? You have a whole gauge on your dash that is totally devoted to the fuel level, right? How the heck did you run out? Didn't you look at it? I think the warning light that we are out of patience is when we become demanding and irritable.

So to fix it, go to the pump – or the source – for love. That is Christ. Say a prayer before you walk into the house, "Lord, let me be loving." Spend time in His Word. Pray to start your day. If you forget to pray in the morning – as we often do because we are in a hurry or just too tired or not in the mood – take a break during the day and just spend it with Jesus. He is your source for love – let Him fill you up.

You don't have to be a love refinery and manufacture your own patience and love; He will give it to you! But just like fuel in a car, you have to take time to stop and fill up. I might sound like a broken record, but you need to spend time with Him each day. Make it your practice to spend at least a few minutes with Him so you have something to pour into your relationship each day!

SHE SAID:

If you set out to write a book about biblical marriage, you are legally obligated to include this verse. Ok that's not really true, but it *is* probably the most common passage of Scripture heard at weddings. It was part of our own wedding ceremony back in 1997.

One of the best tricks I ever heard about processing through this verse was to insert your own name in place of the word "love". As in, Tracy is patient and kind. Tracy is not jealous or boastful or proud or rude. Tracy does not demand her own way. Tracy is not irritable, and she keeps no record of being wronged.

Wow. How am I doing with that? I don't want to be too hard on myself, so most days, not too shabby. However, I can definitely pick out the traits that are more challenging for me for sure.

Here's the thing: Scripture says that God is love (1 John 4:8). God is perfect. His love is perfect. And me? Well, I'm not God. But I *do* have His Spirit living in me, and if you've decided to follow Jesus, then you do, too! I believe God chooses to do life with us because He wants to love people well *through* us, starting with our spouses.

Today, take a moment to pray and receive God's perfect love so you can pass it on to your husband.

HE THOUGHT:

_____
_____
_____
_____
_____
_____
_____
_____
_____
_____
_____
_____
_____
_____

SHE THOUGHT:

_____
_____
_____
_____
_____
_____
_____
_____
_____
_____
_____
_____
_____
_____

DAY 15

Ecclesiastes 4:12 A person standing alone can be attacked and defeated, but two can stand back-to-back and conquer. Three are even better, for a triple-braided cord is not easily broken.

HE SAID:

I have done a few weddings as a pastor. This one is pretty popular as far as verses go in wedding ceremonies. For good reason – it's so stinking good! When I think of standing alone, I can't help but think of elementary school. When you were in school, there was nothing worse than being alone. Sitting at the lunch table alone, being picked last for schoolyard ball, or getting picked on and not having a friend to stand up for you and tell the bullies to shut up – that was the worst. It always feels better to have someone with you in a mess than to be in it alone, right?

I am always able to do more and feel braver when I have a partner in crime. This is why God set up marriage. You are just not as effective alone. You get discouraged easier, you feel more scared alone, and you are less likely to accomplish great things without someone to say, "Hey, we got this!" Even if you fail, you still have someone to look at and say, "It was worth a shot."

God put you with your wife so you can stand back-to-back with her and take on the world! Even if you win at life alone, it doesn't mean as much. If I couldn't look at my wife at the end of the day and say, "Oh my gosh, I can't believe that just happened!" it wouldn't mean jack. We are meant to have a partner.

We are also meant to do life with God. He is the third (or the first) cord that makes us strong together. If you really want your marriage to be unbreakable, make sure you include Christ in it. Worship together, pray together, read Scripture together, and seek Christ together! Your marriage is going to be pretty hard to break if Christ is holding the two of you together. Wow – now that's a strong marriage. Think of some ways that you can bring Christ into your marriage more and more, write it down, and talk to your wife about it!

SHE SAID:

Question: You know what really ticks Satan off?
Answer: Two unified, purpose-filled people who are passionately in love with Jesus and each other.

That's no joke. When we are united with other believers, the devil hates our potential. He strives to attack us and divide us where we pose the biggest threat to the darkness. People who are alone become more vulnerable to discouragement and defeat, so he attacks our marriages, trying to cause anger, hurt, and, ultimately, division.

Jesus calls Satan a liar and the father of lies (John 8:44). This is his tactic. He is relentlessly, brutally, continually LYING to you. Yes, even right now as you are reading this! He wants to wreck your life and destroy your opportunity to walk in victory. Don't buy into his lies. Stand united in the truth!

Think about your marriage. Is there something you believe about yourself or your spouse that just might not be true? Do you have the same fight over and over again? If so, maybe there's a lie you can identify together. Once you know the truth, you can stand together and fight from the place of victory that Jesus died to give you.

89

HE THOUGHT:

_____
_____
_____
_____
_____
_____
_____
_____
_____
_____
_____
_____
_____

SHE THOUGHT:

_____
_____
_____
_____
_____
_____
_____
_____
_____
_____
_____
_____
_____

DAY 16

1 Corinthians 16:14
And do everything with love.

HE SAID:

And do everything with love. Remember that next time you are cleaning the toilet or changing that diaper! Wow, what a powerful concept. What if instead of doing things out of some sort of obligation, you did it out of love?

A while back I was lying in our bed at home and I heard my wife in the bathroom, talking to our daughter. She said, "Please make sure and put the hairbrush back in the drawer where it belongs!" If you have kids, I bet you can relate to this. In that moment I made a decision. Every time I saw that hairbrush on the counter, I would put it in the drawer where it belongs.

91

You might ask, "Why? Why would you do that?" You might be thinking, "Train your kid to do it. Create a system or some way of making sure it always gets put away. Punish your kid every time they forget or create an incentive, etc." I honestly don't know what made me do this except I thought to myself, "I love my wife, and I like seeing her happy and having one less thing to stress about."

So every time I see that hairbrush on the counter, even to this day, I just put it in the drawer. I don't get mad about it. I don't roll my eyes either. I just do it. I have yet to get tired of it. Want to know why I don't get tired of it? Because I choose to do it out of love for her.

When you choose to do everything out of love for your wife, you don't get tired of it. I want to challenge you today to do what you do around your house, and just in general, out of love. When you do that, all those feelings of having to do things out of obligation or because you're "supposed to" will fade away.

I want to challenge you today to write down at least one thing that you hate doing right now. Then pray and make a conscious decision to do it out of love from now on. I bet it will change everything about your attitude toward that thing, and your wife will love it, too!

SHE SAID:

Each of us has a "love language". If you've never heard this concept before, Dr. Gary Chapman discusses them in his book *The 5 Love Languages*. A love language is the way you give and receive affection. My number one love language is "words of affirmation". I like it when Jason tells me nice things like how much he loves me and that he thinks I'm beautiful. It makes my heart go all aflutter. Jason's primary love language is "acts of service". I know that if he has a drawer full of clean socks and underwear, he's one happy camper.

The thing is, I don't always love doing laundry and matching up socks. In fact, I can think of at least a thousand other things I'd rather do. And he doesn't always love having to come up with nice things to say. I mean, how many times does he need to tell me he loves me? He's said it like a billion times in the last twenty years. I should already know by now.

This verse talks about doing everything with love. So even though washing socks is the least romantic thing in the whole world, I will choose to do laundry with love today. Maybe he will choose to write me a love note. Maybe you will choose to give your husband a backrub ("physical touch") or buy your wife flowers ("gifts") or set aside time to eat dinner together without interruption ("quality time").

Think of a gesture you can do today that speaks the love language your spouse needs to hear. Then do it with love!

HE THOUGHT:

_____
_____
_____
_____
_____
_____
_____
_____
_____
_____
_____
_____
_____

SHE THOUGHT:

_____
_____
_____
_____
_____
_____
_____
_____
_____
_____
_____
_____
_____

DAY 17

James 5:16 Confess your sins to each other and pray for each other so that you may be healed.

HE SAID:

How many guys like to admit when they mess up? I don't know too many. In fact, I would say most prefer to overlook our mistakes and move on without much thought. I think most of the time we hope nobody notices, or they just forget about it. I hate doing the wrong thing, and honestly, I hate having to admit I did the wrong thing. But this is the very reason a lot of us go through life wounded and broken. We don't ever tell anyone we messed up!

I saw a video of a former D.E.A. agent who was teaching a class on firearm safety. Here's how it went. He held up a pistol and pulled the slide back. He held it up to show the class, and then he released the slide forward, forgetting the magazine

97

was loaded with bullets. When the slide went forward it loaded a shell into the barrel. Then he pointed the barrel down as he talked and inadvertently pulled the trigger. The class gasped, as you can clearly see the man had just shot himself in the leg. What happened next is crazy! He ignored that he had just shot himself and tried to continue teaching the class! He kept holding the gun and talking as the class totally freaked out. Eventually he stopped trying to teach and got help.

Men do this all the time when it comes to our mistakes and sin issues. We do or say the wrong thing, or have a sin issue in our life, but we refuse to just admit it. If the man in that video hadn't admitted his mistake, eventually he would have bled to death.

Don't be like that. Get help and admit when you mess up. One of the most healing things you can do is look at your wife and say, "I messed up. I lied to you. I yelled at you when I shouldn't have. I did something that was wrong behind your back."

When you can confess your mistakes and pray with each other, healing begins in you and in your relationship. Stop pretending you're perfect because you're not. Only Jesus is. For the rest of us, that means we have to do something to help ourselves heal from doing the wrong thing: confession and prayer.

Is there something you need to tell your wife in order to bring yourself and your marriage to a place of healing? Don't hold back! Do it today.

SHE SAID:

Sometimes people like to fake it, don't we? We slap on a smile and pretend like we've got it all together. We only show our good side when we're having our picture taken. We go about our busy lives pretending everything is perfect, and when someone asks us how it's going, we usually say, "It's going great! I'm just fine."

The thing about sin is that we like to keep it secret.

I'm definitely not encouraging anyone to be a Debbie Downer and walk around talking about or focusing on struggle. In fact, I love that this verse contains a promise! When we confess our sins to each other and pray for each other, it paves the way for healing to begin. How cool is it that God has given you one person with whom you can share your failures?

Jason and I have had some very candid conversations about our sin struggles with each other. And then we pray for each other. We ask God to help us overcome so we can become the best versions of ourselves. I love having someone I can be completely vulnerable with. I mean, don't get me wrong, this is scary at first. Nobody enjoys bringing their flaws out into the light so they can be seen and analyzed. But once you begin to do this as a couple, you experience a whole new level of intimacy.

You can only love unconditionally when you truly know the whole of another person and you accept them anyway.

Is there something that you've been withholding from your spouse? Do you have a sin you keep hidden? Set a time to talk about these things together and pray for each other. When you open up, your healing will begin!

HE THOUGHT:

_____

_____

_____

_____

_____

_____

_____

_____

_____

_____

_____

_____

SHE THOUGHT:

_____

_____

_____

_____

_____

_____

_____

_____

_____

_____

_____

_____

DAY 18

*Matthew 6:33 Seek the Kingdom of God
above all else, and live righteously,
and He will give you everything you need.*

HE SAID:

Ever wake up in the middle of the night worrying about everything? There are times when I feel like the weight of the world is too much for me. I hate that feeling of not having all I need. I wake up thinking thoughts like, "There's not enough money to fix the car and the house and pay all the bills. There's not enough time to finish all the stuff I need to get done at work and home, much less time left over for fun. I don't have the skills I need. I'm not good enough or smart enough to get the job done. I don't have enough love in my tank to give my wife and family."

I hate nights like that. Maybe I am the only one who that happens to, but I doubt it.

Here is what I can tell you: if you are continually seeking Christ and His Kingdom, and seeking to do the right thing, He will always give you what you need. I think in those times when I am worried and full of tension and stress, it's because I am not seeking His Kingdom; I am seeking my own. This verse sounds a lot like a promise.

Here's what I want to challenge you with today: if you feel like you are in need, seek His Kingdom more. Does your marriage feel rough? Spend some more time on your knees in prayer, spend some more time in His Word, spend some more time in worship. You will never find Christ in your own effort. You won't find Him in a self-help book, or in a budget. You have to hit your knees and invite Him into your life consistently. Then do the right thing.

What is He asking you to do? This verse says to seek His Kingdom, and live right.

It's not enough to just seek His Kingdom. He has some stuff for you to do on top of that. I don't know what that is for you, but He does. Take some time in prayer today – real prayer – and ask Him what you are supposed to be doing. Write it down and then ask Him to help you start doing it!

SHE SAID:

One of the biggest things couples fight about is money – where to get it, what to do with it, and why it's already been spent. We all have different ideas about what we deem is valuable enough to invest in. Some of us (ahem, him) could easily blow $300 on new fishing equipment. And some (ahem, me) would rather see some more bling in my jewelry box or shoes in my closet.

Once a person begins a relationship with Jesus, there comes a day when they are faced with a decision: will I trust God financially as well as spiritually? That day for me happened in our garage after a fun, spirited discussion (ok, an argument) with Jason about increasing our giving at church to 10% of our income - returning the tithe to God.

This was a doozy of a fight – in which at one point I loudly declared, "It's a mathematical equation! You can't give more than you have. There's only so much left over after we pay bills!!" (My friends will find this argument extra funny because I, of all people, brought up *math*.)

Long story short, I chose to give our first full 10% tithe that Sunday just to spite Jason and prove him wrong. (For the record, this is not a good motivation for generosity, but God is good, and He still used it to change my heart.) We tithed, saw God's faithfulness, have never quit, and have no regrets. As I write this, it's been over 13 years. As we have stepped out in faith financially, He has always taken care of us, just like He promises in this verse.

I now know the flaw in my garage-argument thinking: God doesn't deserve leftovers; He deserves my all. Now you have a choice to make, too. Together will you choose to financially seek God's Kingdom before your own?

HE THOUGHT:

_____
_____
_____
_____
_____
_____
_____
_____
_____
_____
_____
_____
_____
_____

SHE THOUGHT:

_____
_____
_____
_____
_____
_____
_____
_____
_____
_____
_____
_____
_____
_____

DAY 19

1 Peter 4:8 Most important of all,
continue to show deep love for each other,
for love covers a multitude of sins.

HE SAID:

I remember when my wife and I first met. I really liked her a lot! I did a lot of things to let her know that I liked her a lot! I would say nice things all the time. I would buy her presents, and do nice things for no reason. I never looked for her faults. I liked her too much to even notice.

But what tends to happen after a while in every relationship, is the "new" starts to wear off. We begin to notice things we didn't notice before, even really small things. We stop trying to get her to like us so much. We think, *why should I try so hard? I already got her to like me.* Pretty soon we notice habits of hers that we don't like, and some of her mannerisms might begin to irritate us. If we're not careful, we can start to be really annoyed real quick.

Why does this happen? I think it's because we stop trying to show the love, or even show the like... *I already got the girl, I don't need to work so hard.* Let me share something with you: marriage is a lot of work. Sorry to break it to you, but it is. I wish I could tell you that after five years you can hit cruise control and just coast, but that's just not how it works.

Think of it like this: how do you take care of your car? You have to fill it with gas, oil, and antifreeze. You have to do maintenance and get work done on it or it is not going to last, right? The same thing is true with your marriage. If you forget to put in love, it might just blow up on you. You have to keep putting in some work, because marriage always takes effort.

When your wife knows you work hard to make her feel loved, she feels secure. Also, when you are working hard to show love, you don't let her little flaws and quirky mannerisms bother you. I mean, who cares? You love her!

Write down some ways that you need to show the love today.

SHE SAID:

Have you ever played darts? I think this is how Jason and I spent a good portion of our first year dating. We drank a lot of beer and played a lot of darts. And I'm not trying to brag, but I got pretty dang good at it.

My favorite game was cricket. In cricket, you need to hit specific numbers and bull's eyes before your opponent. I had the form down, and I could usually hit what I was aiming for. But not always.

The word sin just means "to miss the mark". This is like throwing a dart toward the bull's eye and hitting the number twenty instead. There are many ways we all miss the mark every day. Happy thoughts, huh? No one but Jesus is perfect when it comes to hitting the target 100% of the time.

The good news is that Jesus covered your multitude of sins and all the ways you miss the mark with His love. In fact, He shed His blood to wipe your slate clean.

When you remember how deeply you are loved, you can deeply love others. You can overlook the ways your husband misses the mark when you remember how Jesus covers your imperfections.

111

Don't beat yourself or your spouse up for missing the mark. Show deep love instead – the love Jesus shows you   so that you can move forward.

How can you deeply love yourself and your spouse like Jesus today?

HE THOUGHT:

_____
_____
_____
_____
_____
_____
_____
_____
_____
_____
_____
_____
_____

SHE THOUGHT:

_____
_____
_____
_____
_____
_____
_____
_____
_____
_____
_____
_____
_____

DAY 20

*Hebrews 13:4 Give honor to marriage,
and remain faithful to one another in marriage.*

HE SAID:

We live in a society without much honor. Maybe in the past we knew how to show honor, but now it seems like we are a nation where dishonor is more the norm. Watch the news for a few minutes, and I think you would agree. We all seem more than ready to bash someone rather than to look at every other person on earth as someone who was created by God, and is loved by Him.

So when we talk about honor, in my opinion (don't get mad), I don't think we have a genuine concept of what that means. Honor means to hold in high esteem, or to respect greatly. I can say truthfully that oftentimes marriage is not treated honorably. So many times it just seems like a good idea.

"Let's get married. If it doesn't work, oh well, we can try again with someone else, no biggie."

But this verse means it should never be taken lightly; it is to be treated with the utmost respect. Scripture says marriage is to be treated with honor. This means I can't look at my marriage as something casual and unimportant. I should place a high priority on doing the real hard work of making it succeed and flourish.

Stay faithful. Don't look at other women. Don't think ungodly thoughts about the woman next door. Love only your wife. Do everything you can do to make sure that you don't wander off and do the wrong thing. Set up boundaries so that you don't stray.

Men, here is my challenge to you today: look at your marriage with honor. Do whatever it takes to make sure that it is going somewhere good.

For me personally, I don't ride in cars alone or hang out alone with other women. Maybe you need to stop watching certain things on Netflix or TV. Maybe you just need to honor your marriage and start giving it the respect and esteem it deserves.

Write down whatever it is for you, commit to be faithful and honorable, and then pray for God to help you.

SHE SAID:

A few years ago, Jason was flipping through his journal, and he said, "This is cool! Look at the ways God has answered all these prayers." I was like, "Gimme that! You have a prayer list in there? Let me see what's on it." He had written down a bunch of specific goals and prayers he had for our family and our church, and he had been filling in all the ways God answered those prayers.

But there was one prayer toward the bottom of this list that made me laugh aloud. It simply said: *I want to see a bear.*

I couldn't resist – I had to tease him! "What's with this one?" I snickered. "I want to see a bear?" I mocked. And he said, "Yes, I've always wanted to see a bear in the wild, and I've never seen one." Hmmm... okaaaayyy then.

A couple of hours later I was thinking about this again, and God gently whispered something to my soul. He reminded me that He wants to give His

117

kids the desires of their hearts. Ouch. I had picked on Jason for something he actually, truly desired. I mean, he even WROTE IT DOWN as a prayer request! So even though it seemed silly to me, I decided to start praying that Jason would be able to see a bear in the wild, and also that I'd be with him when it happened.

We are called to give honor to marriage, and I had been kind of dishonorable in that moment. We are also called to remain faithful to one another; hence, I chose to make his dream of seeing a bear my dream, too. I decided to be his loyal prayer partner. Because really, why wouldn't I want God to give Jason the desires of his heart?

Today, make a decision to prayerfully fight for and with your spouse in order to help their dreams become reality. This begins with telling each other what you desire, no matter how big or small.

And, go!

HE THOUGHT:

_____

_____

_____

_____

_____

_____

_____

_____

_____

_____

_____

_____

_____

SHE THOUGHT:

_____

_____

_____

_____

_____

_____

_____

_____

_____

_____

_____

_____

_____

DAY 21

Galatians 6:2 Share each other's burdens...

HE SAID:

Here is one of the most wonderful things about marriage – we have someone to share our burdens with. When you say, "I do," you have someone to help you in life. You have someone to talk to about what you are going through. You have someone who can understand your life and all your struggles.

When God created man, He looked at him and said, "It's not good for him to be alone." This is so true! We men are kind of a mess without a good woman. We need a helper – someone who can make us better. I love that I can be there for my wife and that she is there for me.

But one of the things I have noticed is that when Tracy is going through difficult stuff, my empathy gene doesn't always kick in. Does this ever happen to you? You are in a great mood, but your wife isn't. Then you get irritated because she isn't sharing in your joy. A spat follows, and you can't understand why she isn't happy. I think this happens a lot in relationships.

I can think of a couple things that might help with this. Ask her some questions. *Are you doing ok? How can I help?* You might not be able to do anything, but it always helps to know someone is there who is willing to help with your problem. Think about Jesus as He carried the cross. At one point, He was so traumatized and broken that He just couldn't go any further. Jesus needed someone to help Him with the burden, and in stepped Simon of Cyrene.

In the same way, maybe sometimes you could step in and carry something for your wife. Maybe instead of being irritated with her struggles, you could do some dishes or laundry – or just pray for her.

Here is your action step for today: ask God to give you empathy for your wife. Ask Him to help you be strong enough to handle it. Sometimes you won't understand the deep pool that is your woman's heart. But you don't have to understand! You just get to be there to help in any way that you can.

SHE SAID:

The first several years of our marriage were pretty rough, to be perfectly honest. For the first seven years, we weren't Christ-followers, so that was a big enough challenge in and of itself. But on top of that, we worked opposite shifts. I worked days, and he worked nights. Yes, we benefited financially because we didn't have to pay as much for daycare, but we paid the price in our relationship.

It's really hard to be on the same page when a) you don't have the same focus (which is now Jesus, but it wasn't then), and b) the other one isn't around to help share burdens.

It's not like we didn't love each other. We just never saw each other! I felt like a single mom all throughout the week, as it felt as though I was taking on all the parenting by myself. (HUGE shout out to my solo mom friends! You are stronger than you know.) In reality, I wasn't taking on *all* the parenting responsibilities. Jason was the day parent, and I was the night parent. That's a really great recipe for burnout and frustration.

This verse tells us to share each other's burdens. To me, that looks like picking up the slack when the other one needs help.

The cold and flu season is upon us right now in Minnesota. First Jason got sick, and then I did. What I love is that now we work together so well, we intuitively know what the other needs. I took on the chauffeuring and cooking while he was laid up in bed, and he made sure I had soup and Nyquil when I was under the weather. We are getting pretty good at this sharing each other's burdens thing.

Sharing each other's burdens is an opportunity to be gracious like Christ, Who carries all our burdens for us. How can you share the load and show grace to your spouse today?

HE THOUGHT:

_____
_____
_____
_____
_____
_____
_____
_____
_____
_____
_____
_____
_____
_____

SHE THOUGHT:

_____
_____
_____
_____
_____
_____
_____
_____
_____
_____
_____
_____
_____
_____

DAY 22

1 Thessalonians 5:11 So encourage each other and build each other up...

HE SAID:

Some people are just naturals at giving encouragement. I'm pretty sure that is not my strong suit. I am really good at pointing out all the ways you do things wrong, or the things you need to improve. I'm not sure that is always led by the Spirit of God, though. If you are in the same boat, maybe you need to practice your encouragement skills.

I have noticed that most men are really good at using their words to chide each other. We've spent years on the school bus or in the locker room busting each other's chops. We can easily quip about what someone just said and turn it into a joke. We've had a lot of practice.

127

I urge you, men, to only use your words to build up rather than tear down. I challenge you to stop and say something positive if you are tempted to rip on someone. I have personally observed men treating their wives like they treat the guys in the locker room. They use harsh, cutting words and then follow it up with, "I'm just kidding!"

If that's you, you need to break yourself of that habit. There is almost nothing more damaging to your wife than negative words, even if they are said in jest. Your wife needs your words to build her up and make her strong and confident.

I have a job for you to do today, men. From here on out, you're called to be the builder of your wife. This is YOUR job – don't let it fall to someone else. YOU be the one who accepts this responsibility.

Write this down, "I accept the responsibility of using my words only in a positive way to my wife. I will always build her up, not tear her down."

SHE SAID:

I've been told I have the gift of encouragement, so this comes very naturally to me. Here are my pro tips for encouraging your guy.

First, pay attention. You have to notice when your husband needs a boost. Is he acting discouraged? Is he saying things that are negative and defeating? What kind of signals is he sending you? Don't just walk on by when you can see he needs some positive affirmation. Don't blow it off, thinking, "I ain't got time for that!" Make time. Nobody else is going to do it, and if they try, they won't be as successful as you will. Your encouragement is what he craves the most.

Second, you need to know the things that make him feel inferior. When he is struggling or feeling like he isn't living up to the expectations he has set for himself, he feels "less than". When he has to walk into a difficult situation, he needs to know you've got his back. So find out what makes him tick, and then you can preemptively build him up before he even needs to go tackle that hard situation.

Third, you can't do this in your own strength. You need to lean in to the Spirit of God as the source of encouragement. Think about all the times we see Jesus encouraging His disciples. He tells them they will do even greater things than He is doing, He repeatedly tells them not to worry, and He famously calls Peter to walk on water. Seriously! When you read the Gospels, look for all the ways Jesus encourages His followers. He does this out of love and never condemnation. I love that about Jesus!

What can you do to encourage your husband and build him up today?

HE THOUGHT:

_____

_____

_____

_____

_____

_____

_____

_____

_____

_____

_____

_____

_____

SHE THOUGHT:

_____

_____

_____

_____

_____

_____

_____

_____

_____

_____

_____

_____

_____

JASON & TRACY KEECH

DAY 23

John 15:13 There is no greater love than
to lay down one's life for one's friends.

HE SAID:

Here is the deal: Jesus gave His life for us because
He loves us. What an awesome act! It was the
greatest show of love in history. He calls us His
friends. Wow! One of my favorite movies of all time
is *Tombstone*. I can almost quote it line-for-line. In
one of the scenes, someone asks Doc Holliday why
he is helping Wyatt Earp track down the cowboy
gang. His response is, "Wyatt Earp is my friend."
The other guy says, "I got a lot of friends," and
Doc shoots back, "I don't."

I love that loyalty – it's so cool! I love that Doc is
loyal to Wyatt, Jesus is loyal to us, and in the same
way, we need to be loyal to our best friends, our
wives. Tracy is my best friend. I am willing to do
things for her that I won't do for anyone else. I

sacrifice for her because I love her.

At your wedding, two people became one. You committed to be lifelong besties with someone, and here is a hint: it wasn't your best man. If anyone ever accuses you of being "whipped" because you decide to hang out with your wife rather than your buddies, you should smile and say, "YES! My marriage is going good!" If your wife is giving you grief because you spend too much time with the boys, maybe you should pause and ponder how things are going with her, your best friend.

Like I said before, "Happy wife, happy life." At the end of the day, hanging out with the fellas is never as good as the time I spend investing in my marriage. I want you to assess yourself today and see if you need to lay down your life a little more so that your marriage is in a good place. Write down some ways you can sacrifice – or lay down your life – to invest in your best friend and make your marriage strong and happy.

SHE SAID:

I vividly remember the first moment I held our son, our firstborn child, in my arms. He was finally here!

134

Our adorable seven-pound-four-ounce-full-head-of-hair miracle all wrapped up in a little receiving blanket. I said, "Hello," and he looked up at me with wonderment in his eyes at the sound of my voice. And I thought, "Wow. I just met this person, and I would jump in front of a train for him." This is the self-sacrificial love of a mother for her child. The kind of love that makes a Mama Bear growl and bare her teeth at the threat of danger.

That baby is twenty years old now - the same age I was when Jason and I first met. I was reflecting on this memory the other day, and a thought popped into my head: would I jump in front of a train for my husband? After all, I did promise to love him like this.

Jason is my very best friend. Hopefully you can say this about your spouse, too! And hopefully, none of us will ever need to make such a drastic life-or-death decision. But there are small ways we can sacrifice for each other every day. We can even choose to do really hard things out of love, like keeping some of our opinions to ourselves (or maybe that one is just for me). How can you lay down your life to bless your spouse today?

HE THOUGHT:

_____
_____
_____
_____
_____
_____
_____
_____
_____
_____
_____
_____
_____

SHE THOUGHT:

_____
_____
_____
_____
_____
_____
_____
_____
_____
_____
_____
_____
_____

DAY 24

1 Thessalonians 3:12 And may the Lord make your love for one another and for all people grow and overflow, just as our love for you overflows.

HE SAID:

Ok, don't tell Tracy, but there can be times where an overflow of love is not happening. I'm just being honest. It's not her fault. Life just happens, and sometimes we lose focus on what's important. I'm guessing you have times when you don't feel the love so much. I hope I'm not the only one, or I'm going to have to buy a lot of flowers for a lot of days...

Think of the seasons during the year. Some are better than others. In Minnesota, where we live, it can be 70 degrees one day and 0 the next. The weather can change and really mess things up. The good thing is, we know it's "just a season" and a change can/will come. Each season requires a certain response to maintain stability and good health. I think we all experience seasons of drought when it comes to our feelings.

Want to know when I start to notice droughts of love in my life? When I stop asking Jesus to help me to love. This verse tells us that Christ makes our love grow and overflow. He can make your love grow, so go to Him and ask Him to make it grow. Honestly, sometimes you may not feel the love for your wife, and your love could be really small. Ask God to make it grow.

As you feel your love grow, ask for overflow. Here is something beautiful that I have noticed: when my marriage is full of love – if it is overflowing – other people benefit from it! My kids are happier, my co-workers are happier, and since I'm in ministry, all those I minister to benefit from that overflow.

You have to start with Christ. He makes all things grow. He makes all things new. Pray right now for your love to grow and overflow. Write down a prayer of gratitude in advance for His overflow of love.

SHE SAID:

Jason and I used to have a standing weekly lunch date at Applebee's. (I know, we so fancy.) We ate there every Thursday for about 6 months, and we almost always had the same server. After a while, she would stop by just to chat because we were regulars. (And also probably because we believe in leaving great tips!) One day, she said, "I just have to ask… why are you two so happy all the time?"

Pause. It was a golden opportunity to talk about our faith, and it was straight from God. When someone asks you a question like this, it's wise to be ready to share the Good News about Jesus. Scripture talks about always being ready to give a reason for the hope you have (1 Peter 3:15). Don't miss this chance! At the very least, you will be able to plant a seed. And sometimes you'll get to be the one who helps that person meet Jesus!

So Jason replied, "Well, I've gotta play the Jesus card. We're believers, and He has changed our lives!" Then we told her about our church that was right down the road, and we gave her an invite card to come check it out sometime. Simple as that.

Why am I telling you this story? Check out today's

verse. God is the center of our marriage, so we rely on Him to grow us closer together. As He has grown our love for one another, we've become more loving toward other people. Our love overflows to our kids, our friends, the people in our church, and yes, even to the server at Applebee's!

People will take notice when you choose to allow God to grow your love for one another. A lot of people tell us they admire the strength of our marriage. We have a strong marriage because the Lord is our foundation, and He is continually growing our love!

Do you feel like you have love that overflows to other people? If not, return to God. He'll grow that love in you.

HE THOUGHT:

_____
_____
_____
_____
_____
_____
_____
_____
_____
_____
_____
_____
_____

SHE THOUGHT:

_____
_____
_____
_____
_____
_____
_____
_____
_____
_____
_____
_____
_____
_____

DAY 25

Romans 12:10 Be devoted to one another in love. Honor one another above yourselves. (NIV)

HE SAID:

There's that honor word again. Here is the thing about this verse, men: we are to honor (or esteem) our wives above ourselves. When I was single, life was pretty simple. I had the single life figured out. I could eat whatever I want, I knew where all my money was going, and I knew if all the bills were paid. I never had to call anyone to let them know if I was going to be late.

Then when I got married, everything changed. It wasn't just about *me* anymore; it was about *us*. Suddenly I had to learn how to communicate, to watch where those dollars were going, and to call or text if I was going to be late. It was a whole new ball game. You know, I think a lot of married people are still stuck in the single-person mindset.

143

They think they can still do things the way they used to, or the way they want to. But marriage is about honor – about thinking of the other one before ourselves.

If you really love your wife, place her needs above your own. It's scary, I know. We are so caught up in making sure that our needs are met, that it is difficult to look at someone else's needs first. Think of it this way: if I was hungry before I was married, I just ate something. Now when I am hungry, I show honor by asking my wife if she is hungry, too. Then I get food for the both of us. I could just get food for me and let her worry about herself, but if I kept thinking that way, my marriage would suffer.

Here is my challenge to you today: think about the ways you need to start honoring your wife. I'm sure there is some way that you need to do that, even if in your mind you're the husband of the year. Write it down, pray, and ask God to help you grow in that area.

SHE SAID:

I love that word: *devoted*. It means to be committed, loyal, dedicated, constant, and steadfast. This book is called a *devotional* because it's designed to help you be more faithful in your relationship with God and with each other. When we take the time to reflect on Scripture, it makes us stronger as individuals and as couples. When we read together and process what we're learning, it solidifies our bond.

Hopefully you've been spending time every day reading this with your spouse because you want to grow in your commitment to each other. Just as you've set the time aside to study these passages about marriage, will you devote yourselves to one another in love?

I've got to warn you, though – being devoted in love is not something you can just check off your to-do list like, "Cool! I read that thing, and now I don't have to think about it anymore." (Which I really hope you aren't doing, by the way.)

Devotion is stronger than that. When you're devoted to something or someone else, it is not meant to be temporary. Devotion is making a lifelong promise or pledge that no matter what, you're not going to quit.

When things get hard or you're left feeling disappointed at something your spouse said or did, will you remember to remain devoted to them in love?

Today, choose to devote yourself to your spouse and honor them above yourself all over again.

HE THOUGHT:

_____
_____
_____
_____
_____
_____
_____
_____
_____
_____
_____
_____
_____
_____

SHE THOUGHT:

_____
_____
_____
_____
_____
_____
_____
_____
_____
_____
_____
_____
_____
_____

DAY 26

Ephesians 4:15 Instead, we will speak the truth in love, growing in every way more and more like Christ, who is the head of his body, the church.

HE SAID:

Have you ever said something really stupid that resulted in an argument? I know I have. These are the moments you wish you could go back in time, take back the words you said, and say something else instead. You know, something smart like, "You look pretty today!" We all have regrets about the stupid things we've said. But for some of us, our need to speak the truth is so overwhelming that we forget about love entirely.

That's me in a nutshell. I grew up in a house where there were a lot of opinions. And I do mean A LOT of opinions. We never had a problem telling someone else when we thought they were wrong. In fact, we would even offer them the solution too, free of charge. Like a two-for-one special!

Now don't get me wrong, there is nothing wrong with being forward or direct, or simply sharing your mind. But there is always a danger that you are not doing it from a place of love. It used to drive me crazy when I was younger if someone would say something I knew was wrong, even if it was as unimportant as a song lyric. I just felt a compulsion to correct them and let them know exactly what they were wrong about. Sometimes it would lead to really dumb conflicts or arguments.

Unfortunately, this has also happened in the past in my marriage. I would make it my mission to point out Tracy's faults or things I was annoyed about. I just couldn't seem to let it go if I thought she was doing something wrong. And often times, it would lead to an argument. I have learned that I don't always have to speak the truth. I can be quiet, even when I'm right. Sometimes it just doesn't matter! Who cares if she keeps singing that song lyric wrong anyway? I have also learned that the way you deliver the message matters.

Here is what I want you to consider today: if you can't say what needs to be said *in love*, does it really need to be said? Pray that God will give you wisdom for when you *should* talk, and the strength to keep your mouth closed when you *shouldn't*.

SHE SAID:

We had a revelation about our relationship in the last year. Here's the story. We were driving to church on Sunday morning, and Jason was just talking away, unloading all his thoughts about the church service and the weather and the kids and coffee and what was on the radio and Lord even knows what else. I was not feeling it. I've already let you know I'm not really a morning person, and on Sundays we wake up earlier than any other day of the week. So I wasn't being snappy, but I was only giving him one-word responses to all of his many MANY words. I was like, "Yeah." "Cool." "Ok." And I could tell he was becoming frustrated with my lack of response to his enthusiasm.

Finally, I just said, "This has nothing to do with you, I just don't really feel like talking right now."

Doesn't sound like an epiphany moment, does it? But for us, this was huge. I know that Jason is going to accept me no matter what, and sometimes I get so comfortable in our relationship that I let my ugly side come out. Do you know what I mean? It seems as though we give ourselves permission to be cranky with the ones who love us unconditionally, taking them for granted.

In this instance, I chose to speak the truth, but in a very loving way. (I know – I was *so much* like Jesus! Go, me! I am so humble about it, too.) All joking aside, I could have told him the *truth* in this way: "Oh my gosh, are you done talking yet? I'm tired, and all your yammering is completely destroying my peace and quiet."

But we are called to be like Christ – to speak the truth *in love*. I love Jason, so I chose to be calm, loving, and gentle with my words, and because I did, he didn't become upset or offended. (Man – I wish I were this great all the time!)

Scripture talks about how Jesus came to bring us grace and truth (John 1:14). God's truth is always steeped in grace. Choose to be graceful with the truths you need to speak today, especially with your spouse. In this way, you will become more like Jesus.

HE THOUGHT:

_____

_____

_____

_____

_____

_____

_____

_____

_____

_____

_____

_____

_____

SHE THOUGHT:

_____

_____

_____

_____

_____

_____

_____

_____

_____

_____

_____

_____

_____

DAY 27

Colossians 3:13 Make allowance for each other's faults, and forgive anyone who offends you. Remember, the Lord forgave you, so you must forgive others.

HE SAID:

This verse is amazing! I absolutely love it! Why? Because it says to forgive anyone who offends you. We live in such an offended world right now. Facebook and the Internet feed into it, too. The world's philosophy seems to be, if you get mad at someone, just write a scathing review or blog post, or blow up the comments section. We have so many opportunities to live in our offenses nowadays. But God says don't live the offended life. Rather, make allowance for each other's faults.

This means giving others the benefit of the doubt. I decided in the last month or so to not go out of my mind when someone is doing 45 mph in a

155

55 mph zone. It used to bother me so much. It kind of drove me crazy and made me miserable. God reminded me that we aren't supposed to be all ticked off and feeling miserable all the time. If I remember right, His Word says something about living life to the full somewhere... (John 10:10)

And yet, time and time again, we let what other people do dictate how we feel. Remember, no one is perfect – no one – including you! That person may be driving slowly because they don't feel comfortable in the weather conditions, or they have a migraine and are just trying to make it home, or they are grieving the loss of a loved one and just lost track of where they are. My point is this, when it comes to your marriage, why do you let your wife's little faults bug you so much?

Today, accept her for exactly who she is, flaws and all. God forgave you for all your mess (and He continues to) because you aren't perfect either. So be glad that God doesn't get annoyed with you. In fact, He accepts you! He sees you as perfect because you are a Christ-follower. Make the decision to not be annoyed or offended, and to live the forgiven life. It's the best way to live!

SHE SAID:

They say there are two types of people during any conflict: *fight* people and *flight* people. Fight people want to "discuss" the issue until they feel like they've been heard. They don't take the time to cool off when a conflict happens; they immediately jump to venting their thoughts and opinions. At times this can get... loud and heated. Jason is like this. If there's a disagreement, he wants to resolve it right away, even if all our emotions are at their peak and we run the risk of saying harmful things to one another.

This is not who I am. I am a flight person for sure. I don't like to have hard conversations. I hate the chaos of an argument. I despise conflict, so I avoid it at all costs. The problem with that is, when disagreements arise, I don't want to talk about them. I just think to myself, "I'll get over it eventually." The pattern that I used to see in my own life is that I would become offended or annoyed about something, but I would keep my mouth shut in order to avoid the discomfort of conflict. I would stuff all my anger and hurt way down deep inside, and then when the time was right, I'd completely blow up, unleashing months or even years' worth of resentments all at one time.

God tells us there's a solution for these two extremes: forgiveness. If you're like Jason, you can try taking some time and space to breathe for a minute and offer forgiveness in your heart and mind before you come back together to hash everything out. If you're like me, don't let your resentments build up. For example, if I have an expectation that Jason is going to pick up his dirty clothes off the floor, but he doesn't meet that expectation, and I don't address it immediately – boom, resentment. So here's my little trick: I have learned to embrace the chaos of a hard conversation just a little bit. I have to choose to go ahead and speak my mind (in a loving way) as soon as the offense happens or my expectation isn't met. This way, we never have one of those "Tracy becomes angry and hulks out" moments.

Which kind of person are you – fight or flight? Discuss this with your spouse today, and then commit to choose forgiveness and prevent resentments in your disagreements or moments of conflict.

HE THOUGHT:

_____

_____

_____

_____

_____

_____

_____

_____

_____

_____

_____

_____

SHE THOUGHT:

_____

_____

_____

_____

_____

_____

_____

_____

_____

_____

_____

_____

DAY 28

Galatians 5:13 ... serve one another in love.

HE SAID:

Have you ever done the dishes or swept the floor out of love? Chances are, you've mostly done these things because you felt like you had to. A lot of times we do things out of obligation rather than a heart of love. The problem with that is, we can start to build resentments toward the people who aren't helping with whatever it is we're doing.

Can you see how this leads to conflict? In my home, sometimes I can start to feel like a martyr. I start feeling like I should be served and like nobody ever does anything for me, simply because my motivation is off. I can forget very quickly that *we love each other*, and I can forget that the reason why I might do a chore around the house is because I love my wife.

161

Life is busy, time is short, and we can be so tired by the time we get home, that it can be tough to be motivated to serve our wives.

Here is what I want you to do today: make a list of some of the things you do around the house, and leave a space underneath each one. Write down a maximum of five things – maybe they are the things you hate to do the most. Now go back and write, "Because I love my wife," under each one. Then just take a second and pray for a new heart, and a new motivation to help out.

My guess is that as you begin to serve your wife from a place of love rather than obligation, your marriage will get a little better. Your level of frustration will drop, and conflicts will be reduced. Remember, we don't serve each other for the recognition we receive; we do it because we love each other. But, don't forget to recognize when your wife serves you and show her gratitude. I bet that will make her happy!

SHE SAID:

We have an unspoken morning routine that varies just a bit from day to day, depending on who wakes up first. The earliest riser goes down to the kitchen to start the coffee and let the dog out. The next one up feeds the dog, pours two cups of coffee, and brings the cups (and the dog) back upstairs. (I like to start my day with my Bible, coffee, and Black Lab snuggles – don't judge.)

The thing about this routine is that we don't have to coax the other one into doing the coffee making or pouring. We just do it. We serve one another in this simple way every single day. We never had a deep conversation about it. We didn't sit down and plan it all out like, "On Mondays, Wednesdays, and Fridays, you'll do the brewing, etc." Nope. Nothing official. We just choose to do this quick display of love and recognition for each other.

I would guess you probably have similar routines in your own home that you've never even thought about. What are some of the ways you already serve one another in love? How can you take it up a notch today? If you can't think of any ways you serve each other, it's not too late to start! Give a little effort for each other in some area today and watch your marriage flourish and thrive.

HE THOUGHT:

_____

_____

_____

_____

_____

_____

_____

_____

_____

_____

_____

_____

SHE THOUGHT:

_____

_____

_____

_____

_____

_____

_____

_____

_____

_____

_____

_____

_____

DAY 29

James 5:9 Don't grumble about each other...

HE SAID:

I don't know how much more straightforward you can get than this verse. Complaining is so damaging. Think about it: what good does it accomplish? Not a dang thing, but it is such an easy habit to get into. In fact, I think one of the easiest ways to connect with others is by complaining. It's the lowest form of relational connection – to figure out what you have in common through what you both dislike, then grumble about it! But this verse is flat out saying *don't do that.*

Is this you? Do you spend a lot of time complaining or grumbling? Think for just a second, when you sit around the break table at work, are you complaining about your boss or coworkers? When you are on Facebook, are you getting on the

JASON & TRACY KEECH

bulletin board in your local town and talking smack about "that neighbor" or the business that ticks you off all the time?

If this sounds like you, and you're cringing a little bit, your relationship could be in serious trouble. For real, one of the worst things you can ever do is develop a habit of complaining. It is super easy to start complaining about your wife. To sit around and bad-mouth her and just vent a little at work or to your friends about how she spends too much money or doesn't do what you want her to do around the house. Then instead of being filled with joy to see her at the end of the day, you kind of dread it because you've convinced yourself and others that she *just isn't all that great.*

If you spend your time planting seeds of discontent, pretty soon you will reap a harvest of negativity. You can't have a positive life if you dwell in the negative. Change it today! Write out a list of positive things you are grateful for, about your life and your wife. Start to plant seeds of positivity in your relationship, and you will grow goodness.

Make a commitment to only speak positively and to never grumble. If you need to, put the list of positive things somewhere you can see it all the time, and every time you see it, thank God.

SHE SAID:

Uh oh. I can feel a soapbox moment rising up in me. Don't grumble about each other. Please. For the love. Period. End of story. When couples complain or speak negatively about each other, it makes me so sad and upset. Don't you see the blessing you've been given? There are so many people out there searching for the love that you've already found. Why would you choose to be negative and ungrateful?

If conflict is like a burning house, grumbling or complaining is like throwing fuel onto the fire. It does absolutely nothing to improve your situation. It only serves to completely destroy anything that could have been salvaged. What a waste of time!

Ladies, if he makes you mad, talk to *him* about it, not your girlfriends. Don't bad-mouth him to your mom. Don't put him on blast on your social media accounts. Always use the golden rule and treat him the way you want to be treated. I know there are going to be moments when you feel like you just can't resist expressing your disdain, but *you can!* You can resist! Your marriage, your kids, and ultimately, your happiness level and well-being are all going to be better off when you do.

There is someone safe that you can always vent to, day or night, and that's Jesus. He is always there to listen, He'll never leave or forsake you, and He is the best comforter I know. Rather than grumbling, take your worries and cares to Christ in prayer. Unload it all upon Him – He can handle it!

Commit to being positive with your words today, despite any circumstance. The grumbling has got to go, so surrender it to Jesus!

HE THOUGHT:

_____
_____
_____
_____
_____
_____
_____
_____
_____
_____
_____
_____
_____

SHE THOUGHT:

_____
_____
_____
_____
_____
_____
_____
_____
_____
_____
_____
_____
_____

JASON & TRACY KEECH

DAY 30

*1 Peter 3:8 Finally, all of you, be like-minded,
be sympathetic, love one another,
be compassionate and humble. (NIV)*

HE SAID:

Most of us initially are drawn to someone because we have things in common. For Tracy and me, it was Pink Floyd, or music in general. We just have a lot of the same interests. But in the long run, Pink Floyd isn't strong enough to hold a marriage together. More than just like-mindedness, it takes all the other stuff mentioned in this verse.

Be sympathetic. This one can be hard, especially for men. We typically aren't as expressive with our emotions, so we don't know how to sympathize when our wives are expressing theirs. Remember you and your wife are "one". She's part of you, so you'll want to pay attention and care for her when she's hurting. Let her know that you are on her

171

side. Don't ever forget to just be there for her to tell her it's going to be all right.

Love her well. Figure out what makes her feel loved (Notes? Gifts? Cleaning? Back rubs?), and do those things consistently. Go on dates, and figure out new ways to go out and have fun. Surprise her with gifts and cards and spend money on her – she is so worth it. Don't let a day go by without saying you love her, even if you have to text it, or send it via carrier pigeon, say it!

Be compassionate and humble. Remember that you're still not perfect, and don't expect her to be. Be humble enough to know that you're both just doing the best you can. Give her the same grace you give yourself.

My final challenge for you is to hold her hands today or wrap her in a hug and pray for her and yourself. Pray you can love her better. Pray that you can be the man she needs you to be to the best of your ability, with God's help.

Remind yourself every day that you are in this for the long haul, and that you're going to make it. You can do it – I have faith in you. Write a prayer out to God today asking Him for all that you need to make your marriage work.

SHE SAID:

I think this verse is a wonderful way to wrap up the last thirty days! I hope you let these words sink in and that God uses them to transform the way you love each other.

All of you, be like-minded. Have the conversations you need to have to get on the same page about all the small things in life and the big ones, too. The thing that allows Jason and I to be on the same page in many ways is our shared faith in Jesus. Because of the hope we have in Him, we see the world in the same way. Jesus gives people vision. He can help you see things you couldn't see before, like solutions to what you've been struggling with. He can help you see each other with fresh, loving eyes. God gives us a different point of view – He gives us spiritual eyes. That's why the song *Amazing Grace* says we once were blind, but now we see. If life ever seems to be crumbling down around you, stand firmly together on your foundation of faith.

All of you, be sympathetic, loving, compassionate, and humble. Hold on to the things God has taught you about loving each other well over the last thirty days. Keep a firm grasp on what He has said about love and compassion, humility and sympathy.

Remember to be mutually kind and understanding. The truths God teaches us are trustworthy, and they will never lead us astray.

Take some time today to reflect on all you've processed during the time you've been reading through this book, and write down what really stands out to you. Pray together and ask God to help you keep your marriage strong, fresh, and alive. Jason and I are praying for you and asking God to bless you both. May you live happily ever after! Amen.

HE THOUGHT:

_____
_____
_____
_____
_____
_____
_____
_____
_____
_____
_____
_____
_____

SHE THOUGHT:

_____
_____
_____
_____
_____
_____
_____
_____
_____
_____
_____
_____
_____
_____

ABOUT THE AUTHORS

Jason and Tracy Keech have been married since 1997, and they're passionate about helping people find the life change they've found in Jesus. They've been active in ministry at their home church The Crossing (a multi-site church north of Minneapolis) since 2004.

They love date nights, traveling, Mexican food, laughing a bunch, their two amazing kids, and one very special and very spoiled Black Lab.

This is their first book.

Instagram: @JasonKeech @TracyKeech

For more info about The Crossing Church, visit freegrace.tv.

79767922R00101

Made in the USA
Lexington, KY
26 January 2018